WHEN
SUMMER ROSES

by

Hope Robin

Typeset and published by
The National Poetry Foundation
27 Mill Rd
Fareham
Hants PO16 0TH
Tel: 0329 822218

(Reg Charity No 283032)

Printed by
Meon Valley Printers
Tel: 0489 895460

© Hope Robinson 1990

Sponsored by Rosemary Arthur

Cover photo by Celia Rambaut

To C., N., G., and G.

ISBN 1 870556 607

£4.00

CONTENTS

	Page:
Reprieve	1
Old-Fashioned Girl	2
Santander	4
The Great Wagnerian	5
Frontiers In The Mind	6
Reflections For A Ninety Seventh Birthday	7
It's Complicated	8
Radical Plot	9
Island Invitation	10
Meanwhile	11
Chrysanthemum Throne	12
Consider	13
Life's Like That	14
What Time Is It?	16
Quite The Reverse	18
Cost-Effective	19
Me And Mine	20
I'll Never Know	21
From Another Island	22
Gone	23
Still Learning	24
October - Bar Rema	25
Nerja Thoughts	26
Car Crash	27
The Russian Connection	28
Words Make A Difference	29
How Right Can You Be?	30
Meeting	31
The Eyes Have It	32
Sobornost	34
Durovernum Cantiacorum	35
It's All One	36
Unequal Contest	37
To Whom It May Concern	38
El Capistrano	39
It Happens	40
Birds On The Brain	41
Los Jardineros	42

REPRIEVE

My mother died last night,
I knew the dawn
would find her gone forever
and I dreaded it.

My nine year old,
as if I were her child,
cradled my head,
comforted my tears
and said
"She'll be all right.
I know."

I've lost my mother
but I don't feel motherless.

OLD-FASHIONED GIRL

She was the youngest,
she was plain.
Her pretty sister
danced home with the latest waltz.
"Teach me!" she begged.
"I haven't time!" whirling away
to show her friends.
Music was her talent,
Chopin her joy,
she played, she practiced,
how she would have loved to train!
Duty intervened at seventeen.
Her mother took to bed - the family 'heart!
(She lived to ninety-three).
She helped her father in the church,
she led the Bible-class
taught in the Sunday-School,
sang in the choir.
The organist was young. They fell in love.
"Marry? Impossible! You're needed here."

She ran the house; she nursed.
The maid she had was flighty,
ending up in court.
She had to go as well. She heard the charge
"a common prostitute, soliciting"
but all she saw that day
was the jade coat in the dock.
Since when
she could not bear that shade of green.

She had her garden, she was active, strong.
She weeded, planted, watered,
pruned the hedges, mowed.
When the summer roses bloomed
she sat her mother in the fragrant air,
dreaming about the little car she never had.
But Chopin still was hers.
Often she played, her fingers stiff -
Through all she had her faith.

At length her mother died. She was bereft,
the seeming purpose of her life had gone,
also the tiny pension.
She could not keep the house,
the garden that she loved.
They had to sell the lot
for her to have a room with strangers,
who were kind enough.

She never once complained,
nor blamed her God.
She only asked Him
if He had forsaken her
and asking, died.

SANTANDER

Green against blue,
palm tree and tamarisk,
tamarisk and palm,
wind northerly, warmed
by the misted Spanish sun.
Atlantic waves
falling for ever,
white on tawny far-stretched sand.
I'm glad I came.
I pick the heather at my feet.
It grows at home,
purpling the moors,
those battlefields of long ago
whose mosses once ran red.
This lovely land,
inhabited since history's pre-dawn
by bloody-handed man,
lives on.
Unknowing yet,
the dark-eyed frilly babies,
pushed in Sunday prams
past rusting guns emplaced,
past stark memorials -
TODO POR LA PATRIA
past legless men
whose smiles pierce like a sword;
past begging widows,
wraiths of black
among the summer-coloured café crowd,
thin hands outstretched.
I view the sprig I hold.
Each bell is perfect.
In such a world as this
how can it be?
I only know
poets are remembered here
their faces set in stone
among the trees,
their thoughts alive.

THE GREAT WAGNERIAN
(For Reginald Goodall)

Old age was not for him.
He's gone to join the gods;
He knew them all,
on earth they were his intimates.

He never sought for power.
It was bestowed on him,
it was his gift.
He used it all his life
not to impose or dominate
but to command
from true musicians.
Music so glorious, so pure,
that all who heard,
would love it
as he did himself.

He's with the immortals now.
Because of him
something of us becomes
immortal too.

FRONTIERS IN THE MIND

I read the menu by the plate,
just printed words
and numbers on a card,
shall I have 6 or 8?
Then suddenly
my palate tingles
I can taste the taste
and see the lovely food
all in my mind.
How now to choose between
the trutta or the scalopine?

My letter, not yet posted,
says "Should we separate?"
Already, in my mind,
closeness is gone,
our differences
no longer stimulate
but infiltrate
like cracks eroding
parched and sterile land.
Should a flash-flood spring,
swelling to life again
what seems so dead,
I'll know the green,
the burgeoning,
first in my mind.

The great discoveries too,
the leaps of science
are first in the mind.
Once every century or so
a genius lives.
Others, in the ensuing years
spend all their time
in working out, for lesser men,
what was the frontier crossed.
For in his mind
with his acuity
he saw the discontinuity
of *what must be.*

REFLECTIONS FOR A NINETY SEVENTH BIRTHDAY

With Dorrie it is different.
We didn't choose each other,
There's nothing inexpressible
there's nothing that's ineffable,
she's simply there.
I'm learning every day
that I can care.
There is no need
for it to be reciprocal
and yet I think it is.

Sometimes I'm apprehensive
of growing old and ill
and wonder how I'll cope.
With Dorrie it is different.
She's not afraid at all.
She hasn't time, she has
so many things to think about.
- Will black stockings make
  her legs look slim?
- Can the gardener see her dressing?
- She needs another lace-trimmed petticoat.
- Will this necklace match her blouse?
- Where is her silver basket for
  her fruit I've brought?
- That picture should be higher.
- Her plants need watering.
- The birds are waiting for their crumbs.

Each moment's full.
That's always been her way.
It's no bad recipe.

IT'S COMPLICATED

We like to think we're rational,
but if you've ever seen
an infant in frustrated rage
thrashing around
destroying what he can,
you are relieved he's not a full grown man.

I know a man of peace
(Military Cross, he wears a cassock now)
who cries, when righteously aroused,
"I'd like to put a bomb beneath...!"

You think the really old
have no more fire?
Caged as they are
in impotence
they feel frustration every day
as keenly as you feel desire.
I overheard a cry
to a youthful, thwarting nurse
"If you say that again
I'll murder you!"
She meant it too.

RADICAL PLOT
(after Paustovsky)

>He stood beside his vegetable plot
>and said "This also
>is a way of life.
>Fight for freedom
>if you will,
>reform your fellows
>if you can,
>grow tomatoes.
>Everything has merit,
>everything has cost."
>
>"What is that supposed to prove?"
>
>He said "It proves the need
>to tolerate, to understand.
>freedom has no other key."

ISLAND INVITATION

Red tomatoes,
okras, beans,
soft cassava,
pumpkin, greens,
lettuces with curly edges,
avocados cut in wedges.

Crawfish in its armour-plating,
grouper, fried while you are waiting,
entire, a handsome margate fish
grape-fruited in a spicy dish,
with dilly mayonnaise
and home-baked bread.

Ripe bananas small and neat,
fresh pineapple, crisp to eat
sweet papaya's sunset slice.

A centre-piece to feast your eyes,
rioting hibiscus lies,
new this morning, fresh today,
deepest crimson, palest grey.
Fluted scarlet, frilly brown,
sugar pink and cinnamon,
purple with a yellow trim,
golden with a rosy rim,
stripy red, magenta, blue,
pearly white - picked just for you.

In England it's mid winter.
Can't you stay?

MEANWHILE

The tunnel's dark,
can't see the way ahead,
can't see the light
that should be at the end,
if there is one.

So let me think
of lively little fish
that live (I'm told)
in just one lake alone
beneath the ground
where light is never known.
They're pale,
they're eyeless for
they have no need
of sight;
but they
are quite all right.

There's nothing darker
than the ocean floor
with its abyssal deeps
where new rock swells
up from the molten core
into the vents.
Round them cluster
fauna never seen before,
quite different,
which have no need of sun
for there is none.
They thrive on sulphur
very well; they grow
to six feet long.

My tunnel's dark,
but O! my thoughts are free
to roam the world
where there is more,
much more,
than I shall ever see.

CHRYSANTHEMUM THRONE

He was no military man.
He chose a planter's life
and came to love the East.
When his estate was over-run
by the Imperial Japanese,
they took him:
we heard no more
for years.

He came back from the prison camps.
We recognised him by his smile
that had survived in hell.
His only comment was
"I lost my kilt."

His life was peaceful now,
watching his children grow
among familiar Scottish hills.
But still he never spoke
of what he knew.
No word was ever said.

When he was dead,
I sat beside his widow in the kirk,
watching the wreaths pile high,
the blooms of autumn
yellow, rust and white.
An anguished whisper caught my ear
"It's terrible! Nobody knows.
He couldn't *bear* chrysanthemums."

CONSIDER

Shopping today
inside my local pharmacy,
close to the great cathedral gate,
I found among my purchases
a leaflet, telling all I need to know
about *HEADLICE*.

When Thomas Becket died
the legends say
the lice streamed out.
His cooling body signalled
it was time to leave.
Without his vital warmth
they could not live.
This revealed to those who knew
he really mortified his flesh.
Godliness meant so much more to him
than cleanliness.
Both of these were difficult
in medieval days.
Only the latter's easy now.

On tiled and tropic bathroom floor
I watched the ants retrieve a flake of skin -
my skin, now theirs.
They carried it away, I thought, triumphantly.
A sudden jolt like this remonds;
our bodies are not ours alone,
we're colonised, inside and out
by forms of life not fully known.
Some are benign; some do us fatal harm
and seldom can we choose.

This new perspective
brings a new humility,
but godliness
is still far off from me.

LIFE'S LIKE THAT

My contract typist
types my work herself.
Her busy bureau's full,
machines and girls,
both large and small,
flying fingers,
keys chattering,
chairs clattering,
sheets fluttering.
The calm centre –
she controls it all.

When she has a moment
she will talk
of honeysuckle,
exotic, Japanese,
breathing exotic perfume
round her door,
(does honeysuckle still grow wild
and scented in the Scottish glens?)

Today we met outside.
I would have passed
but for the smiling eyes.
Crash-helmeted,
breeches and leggings
black leather jacket.
She could have landed from the sky
not just a bike.
I couldn't help the question
"Have you learned to fly?"
"No" she answered
"How I wish I had!
Shall I tell you
what my *real* ambition is?
– to fly a *spitfire*!

Modern planes are things;
spitfires are romance
- with wings!"

We parted, longing,
she for her fighter's cockpit.
I for my words to soar.

WHAT TIME IS IT?

I have no watch.
I had to hand it in,
without it I am lost.

This is the city,
birds don't wake me
with a song.
I have to guess the minutes
for my egg.
How long have I
been sitting over coffee?
- at least the toast pops up.
The postman comes at eight
- but maybe not today,
maybe he's late.
I'm helpless, I'm adrift,
a dozen times
I'll have to say
"Excuse me, what's the time?"

Once I had no need of clocks.
I could distinguish night from day,
I knew when I had pain
and when relief.
Familiar faces dimly came
and went. I didn't care.
The faces that I wanted,
the hands that nursed
then were always there.
Time had no meaning any more.
One day I found
that I could lift my head
up from the pillow
and look across the further bed.
Dazzled by light I saw
beyond the window there
a full and leafy tree.

Now I could swear
that when I came in here
the blackened empty branches bare
tossed in the wintry wind.
I know the time it takes
for buds to swell, unfold,
unfurl until at last
their banners fill
a window with triumphant green.

What time is it?
It's spring!
The winter's past
and I shall see
the summer once again.

QUITE THE REVERSE

We talked till late.
My friend confided
that his father must
have had a bitter life,
for bitterness was all he knew,
eroding, negative.
Even as a child
he felt expatriate.

Once, when small,
his father stood him on a table top
commanding "Jump! I'll catch you!"
then took his outstretched arms away.
My friend remembered how he fell
and through his tears he heard,
"You have to learn, trust nobody."

I know my friend;
the scars remained.
But did his father
realise that day
another lesson learned
was how to be betrayed?

COST-EFFECTIVE

I was not ignorant at birth
nor did I come a stranger.
Even if unwelcome
I was still equipped for earth.

My infant body knew its job,
balanced electrolytes,
controlled the nutrient flow,
levelled essential hormones,
I walked, I talked, I grew.

Before I learned what lovers did
or wondered what went on in mother's bed,
(they never thought I listened on the stair)
before such time, my body knew of bliss,
no one taught me.
The world was full of things
that touched and pressed me here and here
and unexpected joy took wings.
Had I then ever innocence?
Or did I lose it when I left the womb that night?

Perfection's classical, but not for me.
The ancients disapproved of ecstasy.
They wanted to believe reason
was always in control.
We know today
reason is but ever passion's slave.

It's worth the price –
the loss of innocence –
for bliss. Some say
the gates of heaven are like this;
others, the gates of hell.

ME AND MINE

My body's mine,
though some of it's outside,
my tears, my sweat,
sometimes my blood,
my hair and toenails
once they're cut and swept.
(A sacred King had all his clippings kept)

I saw today
two laughing children. Unbelievably,
he had her heart, hers was replaced.
Yet as I watched them at their play
there was no doubt
that each had firm identity.

We must be more
than just a sum of parts.
My muscles serve my will,
events inside my brain
grant me my skill,
there's some possessiveness
that unifies:
My body's mine.
But who am I?

I'LL NEVER KNOW

You shut your eyes and never looked again
nor spoke, except to breathe my name
over and over. I leaned to catch it.
Suddenly, with all the mortal strength
that still remained
you held me close.

I found myself
before our window. Dawn was on the sea
whose early tide rolled softly up the sand.
What right had it to flow and swell?
It should have ebbed.
For you were not asleep but dead.
What right my heart to flow and swell,
to be alive instead?

Alive to dress you. Already you were strange,
your flaccid veins, the vital tension gone,
marbling the body that I thought I knew.
Your mighty engine
shrunk like any little boy.
I'm glad I am alone.
No other eyes shall see you in this change.

Whose eyes some day
will gaze on me?

FROM ANOTHER ISLAND

Winter solstice in the Isles of Spring.
The sun goes down and stands
and never moves.
La Gomera etches on its red,
black as the basalt rock,
black as the swelling sea.

Our lamp-lit room is quiet,
our balcon open to the dark
and Chopin plays.
The Nocturne mingles with
the listening night.
Our longing love confirms
we cannot die...

    ... but we were wrong.
All that was years ago.
The sun has stood and moved
so many times. Yet
Chopin plays and I
remember you.

GONE

I know you've gone. The taxi came
I heard you slam the door.
By now you're miles and miles away,
I don't know where.

Your scarf was hanging in its place
when I came home tonight -
But I remembered with a pang
you left it in your haste.

Later in our empty room,
exhausted in my chair
I started - surely that's your key?
No-one was there.

STILL LEARNING

He was as an elder o' the Kirk,
in Sabbath black, with sombre tie,
his rosy face composed,
but not his twinkling eye.

When he retired, they left
for England's sunny south,
to join their only son
and help him on his farm.

On holiday from school
I came to stay,
'a little bit of home.'
All this was new to me.

His wife came back
from shopping in the town
with something in a box
not for herself
for she was frugal still -
only for him.
"He does enjoy them so!"

I watched, incredulous,
as he demolished every bite
his rosy face wreathed with delight
reflected in her joy.

Reflecting, I now understand
that love can be
the biggest cream filled bun
for tea.

OCTOBER - BAR REMA

The pile of emptied winkles grows,
Black as the bread is white -
The sparrows chirp for crumbs.
Intricate whorls,
Gathered while we slept,
Fresh from the rocks,
Fresh as the simple wine.

Empty the shore beneath the mounting sun.
Empty horizon marking sky from sea.
Still moments of accord
Between me and myself,
Between myself and thee.

NERJA THOUGHTS

So many years your life has been your own.
You've made your choices, carried out your plans.
I didn't need to know. You managed all alone.
Yet while I never thought us far apart,
I knew that many miles stretched in between.
I felt the distance in my heart.

I cannot quite believe it here.
Your house is in my view. So near.
That I could walk across to you.

CAR CRASH

One second left for fear,
then agony engulfs;
But I can think and breathe
and suffer, I am alive!

Days on and shattered,
they tell me
that it needs a surgeon's skill
to make me mend.
Why am I so afraid?

It's not the dark,
for every night since I was born
I've gone to sleep without a qualm
and never thought
that morning wouldn't come.

My body knew
just how to draw the lids
down on my eyes,
decelerate my heart-beat,
quiet my pulse,
deepen my breathing
and reverse it all
when it was time to wake again.

This is quite different.
My sovereignty I have to yield
to those into whose hands I pass
and they will loosen all the ties
binding myself to me,
that I may neither think nor feel,
nor hear, nor see,
Oblivion.

THE RUSSIAN CONNECTION

I looked away.

Your eyes were full of tears.
But not because the words were mine.
Paustovsky wrote them - stranger to us both,
Suddenly so close, so fully understood.

The poet knows, if he can write his grief,
That in another country, after he is dead,
A reader, pierced by what he said,
Will weep - and not in sorrow but relief.

WORDS MAKE A DIFFERENCE

Say it, while it can
Still be said.
Only the living talk,
Who hears the silent dead?

A flowering tree,
The touch of skin,
Confirm identity.
But there are words
I have to hear
(Just one or two
Will quite suffice):
"You've passed."
"I do."
"Goodbye."

HOW RIGHT CAN YOU BE?

Surely I've seen her face before
beneath the headline, 'GREENHAM WIRE'?
So round her cheek inviting touch,
so blonde the straggled strand of hair.
Her mouth is set, soft lips compressed,
her eyes are narrowed and can give a clue
to deep determination and belief,
come daily hardship,
come the final test.
I look and wonder idly why
the battle cap she wears says U.S.A.

I read the print again.
A Greenham Woman, yes
but on the *inside* of the mesh:
Flight-Lieutenant Dawn
age twenty-four,
knowing her place, her task, equipped and trained
ready to press the button on command
- it's labelled EXECUTE.

"It's not a job you'd do unless
you're sure the reason's right."

Outside the fence they say the same.
Who then is wrong?

A traveller came and stood
above the Thracian plain
where once a battle raged
that sealed his country's fate in blood.
"God was on both sides, else
how could he be our God," he said.

Who would be God?
It's hard enough
to just be Man.

MEETING

I never thought that I was white
Until black woman called me so.
She did not grudge me coming here,
She did not wonder when I'd go.

I breathe the air beneath her sky,
Her sunshine blesses me each day.
This isle that is her only home
Is home to me throughout my stay.

Black woman, if we ever meet
Some morning in an English lane,
May I with unassuming heart
Make my accepting welcome plain.

THE EYES HAVE IT

My dog's embarrassed
confronted by my gaze
he shifts his eyes and turns his head both ways.
My cat's secure.
She reads me like a book
and stares me out. I blink before her look.

Eyes can have power and controlling range.
In our pre-jumbo flights
I had to see the approach.
How could the pilot bring us safe to land
without my eye's command?

Eyes can be terrible. I read a tale
of where a criminal was built into a wall
and how the wretched mason, sweating, stone by stone
entombed, relentless, the still living man.
And how, when he had reached the victim's face,
he smashed the eyes in, not to meet that gaze,
before he put the final brick in place.

I watch my fisher's boat
go out beyond the reef,
beyond the shelter of the land
to wrest adventure from Atlantic's teeth.
Such challenge could not be ignored.
An elemental wave,
a watery wall
falls on the fragile craft.
Nothing but sea and blinding spray.
I dare not take my eyes away.

"As long as I can watch you'll be all right.
My eyes shall pluck you from
the killer sharks, the cruel sea, the rocks,
as long as I can watch."

Now, where my eyes might fail or flinch,
my movie lens, dispassionately accurate,
continues to record each painful inch.
I summon all my skill.
I'm doing something if I let it roll.
I call upon my will.

Within my sights a bobbing head.
Then two, then three, then four.
That's all of them!
They're safe! They're striking for the shore!

End of event; end of my reel;
I close my camera then
I race to meet their eyes
again, again.

SOBORNOST

Half-serious, half-envious, I said
"When you come back
bring me a little bit of Russia!"

My friend remembered
and put into my hand
gabbro from Tbilisi,
red and palest grey
basaltic lava from Sevan
tufa and obsidian –
Armenian rocks long cold and calm,
lastly, banded black on rose and white
gneiss that sparkled in the light,
innocently bright.
But not the human history,
for these were chips of cobbles from the court
of the dread Peter and Paul,
Leningrad's most fatal prison fort.

I hold them in my palm.
They could have come from anywhere –
there were no frontiers when the earth was made,
but they are Russian,
harsh, archaic, beautiful.
So real they speak to me,
not distantly, but here.

DUROVERNUM CANTIACORUM

My neighbour
brought me grapes today
cut freshly
from his greenhoused vine.

Twenty centuries ago,
barbarian outpost of Imperial Rome,
our climate made
the legionaries feel at home.
So baths and villas,
temples and palaces
were built
and vineyards flourished
in the British sun.

From ancient times
the grapes, the vines
were icons
of a Mediterranean life.
With stalking hunger rife
joy and oblivion
were in the wine.

The Israelites, we learned,
marched in the dust
for forty years
to reach the Promised Land.
What child who ever sat
inside a northern Sunday School
forgets the picture of
the *Grapes Of Eshcol,*
that bending pole
on brawny arms
of curly-bearded spies,
triumphant, underneath
the swaying purple pyramids?

Reflectively, I eat my grapes.

IT'S ALL ONE

Childhood holidays
were spent entirely by the sea.
From Arran, out past Sanda Isle
my father pointed the horizon's gap.
"That way,
there's no more land
until America."

Beneath the moon
the tides that ebb and flow
are, at the equinoxes
full and high.
Each wave as it recedes
draws down the gravel on the sand,
soft sibilant
of unrelenting change.

I find the land-locked country strange.
It disappears into the dark.
And night's deep throat
swallows each house and path and tree
unless the sky is bright.

It's rhythm isn't mine,
the yearly turning and the slow
approach of seasons.
In the daylight fields and crops
look just the same
as they did yesterday,
unchanged.

I like to think there is no solid earth.
Tectonic plates that bear the continents
float on the oceans
and arose from there.
the shells on Kangchenjunga show
what's now so high
once was as low.
The polar ice is melting
a little every day
as the earth returns to sea.

UNEQUAL CONTEST

Each day the gipsy stood
outside the main cathedral gate,
accosting tourists entering
or coming out,
importuning with her sprigs
of stachys, white and green
that could so easily deceive,
especially a young embarrassed man
who paid to get away
before she fixed it on his coat.

So, as she thrust a sprig at me,
I said "That's not white heather!"
"Did I say it was?
It's *luck* I'm selling!"
She didn't need to curse;
she had outwitted me
and that was worse.

TO WHOM IT MAY CONCERN

Your teenage son.
He was among
the fortunate.
He went on the school excursion.
But he, came back.

Cliffs did not claim him,
nor the frozen screes,
nor any foreign sea,
panic suddenly aboard.

"I'll never let him
go again," you say.
You brought him up;
you've had your day.
Tomorrow's choices
will be his alone
you may not save him
from the consequences,
not even if
you give your life.

Be brave, not fearful,
for your heart will recognise
that your mind
already knows.

EL CAPISTRANO

Mimosa, eucalyptus,
tamarisk and pine,
tulipan, palmetto,
ivy's trailing twine -
green backdrop for the spilling shades
of bougainvillea's banners,
thunbergia's cool cascades,
bignonia's blaze,
plumbago's petalled waves.

The morning glory climbs,
the pendant lily hangs
among geranium clusters
bright correopsis shines,
hibiscus blooms with canna,
fuschia with phlox,
rose and starry jasmine
perfume all the walks
while softly in the shadow
the tinkling fountain drops.

There, and there, an ancient olive tree
speaks of the past.
Fruited and gnarled.
Preserved from groves that once alone possessed the slope.

Only in Andaluz, I think, can such things be.
Why do I feel
that they are here for me?

IT HAPPENS

I hung the picture on the wall.

Dark rocks against a dazzling sea,
fringed palm trees etched,
mysterious misty outline of a shore,
familiar, yet compelling.

The eyes of friends who visit me
are drawn as well.
They say "I do like that! Where can it be?
What a marvellous sunset!"

"Sunrise," I murmur.
"Oh, of course!" they cry.
"How talented he is,
artistic, dedicated,
disciplined - and more
to rise and photograph like this at half past four!"

Later I saw him:
"I'll tell you how it was," he said.
"I had been out the night before,
I drank too much
and stumbled home.
I couldn't sleep, I left my bed,
retching and sick,
then grasped the door
that opened from my balcony, facing east."

"The radiance made me lift my head.
It filled the air, the sky, the sea,
a glory flaming from the rising sun to me,
I was part of it,
as if I'd prayed all night for such a dawn,
as if I'd wrestled with an angel
for such beauty to be born."

BIRDS ON THE BRAIN

I've often wondered, so this letter said,
about those blooming doves.
For everywhere I go I see them,
singly or in droves:
on ties, on scarves and posters.
On Christmas cards and bags,
modelled in stone, in plastic,
in plaster, wood or rags.

I'll tell you something that I think I should:

I've bred them,
not like Noah with his only pair,
but scores and scores
and so I'm sure they're free
to fly just when they wish.
They have abundant water, food and resting space
yet none are so destructive,
aggressive unprovoked
and always bent on mischief.

None are so keen
on territorial fights,
striding rough-clawed
across their neighbour's rights.
They wreck each others' nests,
hacking to death
the helpless chicks
with vicious beaks.

Quarrelsome, cross-grained,
bottom of the poll,
totally unsuited
for any peaceful role.

Justice, Compassion?
That's the work for men
- not birds!

LOS JARDINEROS

"A garden is a lovesome thing..."
especially in England.
But there is no monopoly.
Maybe you have seen
what can be done in Spain?
- a garden filled
with stones
untouched by artifice,
rounded only by the sea,
each different,
except in size,
planted - *there* was the art -
in intersecting rows
in such a way
that the effect
was stunning.

My *Monstera* is quite
Deliciosa, for it grows
and grows, from
pot on the table,
then on a stool,
now down on the floor,
yet still it grows.
Another leaf unfurled,
just one
and it will reach the roof.
What's to be done?

If this were Spain
the builders would
have made the ceiling with a hole
so that the garden could come through
as if invited.